A Pound of Cure

A Pound of Cure

poems

Edward Wilson

Cider Press Review
San Diego

A POUND OF CURE

Cider Press Review
PO BOX 33384
San Diego, CA, USA
ciderpressreview.com

First edition
10 9 8 7 6 5 4 3 2 1 0

ISBN: 9781930781672
Library of Congress Control Number: 2024946873
Cover image: *Hopfgarten,* Lyonel Feininger (1920) [Public Domain], courtesy Minneapolis Institute of Art via collections.artsmia.org, https://collections.artsmia.org/art/1268
Author photograph by Drake White
Book design by Caron Andregg

Winner of the 2024 *Cider Press Review* Editors' Prize Book Award: CIDERPRESSREVIEW.COM/BOOKAWARD.

Printed in the United States of America
at Bookmobile in Minneapolis, MN USA.

For my teachers.

Acknowledgments & Thanks

As you see, this book is for my teachers. So many. Here are a few: Grace Wells, Otto Klein, Paul Camplin, Howard Carter, Bob Detweiler, Peter Meinke, Pat Korb, Gordon Bigelow, John Frederick Nims, John Ciardi, Hiram Williams, William Meredith, Shirley Cunningham, Starkey Flythe, Philip Morseberger, Jerry Cullum. Robert Bly's poem "Gratitude to Old Teachers" comes to mind. When you read it, I am sure you will remember your teachers as I do mine.

Some of the poems in this collection first appeared in the magazines cited, often in earlier versions:

Beloit Poetry Journal: "Lot's Wife"
Cider Press Review: "Snow," "January from a Window at Sunset," "March"
Festschrift for Peter Meinke (2019): "After an Old Chinese Poet"
The Georgia Review: "Tenant House II, 1960 (The Morris Museum of Art)," "Dream Dreams"
The Midwest Quarterly: "The Cunning to Get Near Enough"
Narrative Magazine: "My Civil War," "Redwoods up the North Coast"
Poetry: "Fingers," "The Living Corpse"
Southern Voices: Fifty Contemporary Poets: "The Long View," "Sometimes a Day Gets Lost"
The Southern Poetry Review: "Indian Summer," "A Photograph of Mandelstam at 31," "Wishbone"

Contents

III

Luna Moth

On the way back from
a movie at the *Palace,* under
the streetlight at the corner
of the square where
the courthouse dome dreamed
statutes, writs, and codes,

I thought at first
it was a cast-off bit,
a scrap of paper in the gutter,
not the lost leaf
from an enchanted tree.

Wings like curves swallows
carve from startled air.
A green—ethereal—
I'd never seen on any girl
in school, no woman wore
on the sidewalk or in a pew.

It took its time in that pale circle
skittering—again—then still.
But it could not find a stairway
back up to the light.

I did not know
it had no mouth, that it would
never live to see the dawn,
could sense another moth
six miles away, that
I would see it perfectly
from forty years.

I

In the Pines

—for David Dickey

These trees,
thickened mist. Rising,
paling away—like a cathedral
before someone thought of
piling stone on stone.

The empty stand you've left,
the pointless Winchester forgotten
in your hands—excuses
for being here.

Shafts of early light,
thick enough almost
as spider silk to snap
across your cheek.

Needle fall whispering
around your boots, a finger
to the lips, telling you how,
the way to move

downslope where
the creek tangles and steams.
The little buck that walked
under your sights catches
your scent and snorts.

Far off, a crow hacks out
the single syllable of his liturgy.
As if you needed a priest.

Guided Tour

Museums for cotton,
monuments to rice and indigo—
west to the river, from here
to the coast. Statues of those men
pose in the parks, in public squares,
esteemed of grass.

They owned the air—
the ledger, ink, and pen
that wrote your name. Doled
out the light. Clenched the dust
you asked leave to sweep.
And when you slept, garnisheed
the scraps of dreams.

Those houses still loom—
icebergs above live oaks,
columns white as tusks.
You can see the marshes, fields
stretching away from those porches
where they, their sons,
their wives and daughters too,
watched *theirs* spread out like ripples,
like a rock thrown in a pond,
from *have* to the edge of *want*.

Up north, they did it differently.
Hid the bills of sale.
But no matter what the accent,
the language is the same—
the one with no word for *enough*
and a thousand synonyms for *mine*.

Tenant House II, 1960—William Christenbery

—Morris Museum of Art

If you were born down here
like me, about the same time,
you will have seen it—
wind in your face like a dog
from the back window of your father's Buick—
alone in that field, beside the single
Chinaberry tree, forgetting its paint,
rotating slowly as you drive away.

But you won't have been inside.
For that, you'd have to read Agee's
anguished book and see what Evans
saw and shot, what their editors
chose not to print.

But that's not this.
To see that shack like this
you have to lace your boots up
in the dark, dip water from the bucket
like a blind man, taste the tin. For breakfast
remember last night's beans.

Heat in the dirt outside's a prophecy
as light begins to whet the pines.

This is not work—not a garage,
a store, an office with a roll-top desk
under a lazing fan. This is violence
drawn out like sorghum poured,
measured brutality, torment endured.

And if you do, as the trees
go black again, you will have left
most everything between those rows.
Kept just enough to stand and see it
for the beast it is, squatting
in that crazed landscape.

A last hungry thing. Its patient
doorway black, flung wide like jaws,
and you with nowhere else to go.

Slightly Before You Were Born

The club is hot. The music
serpentine, caressing. West Nashville

while the war is on. So much smoke
the jacket in your closet remembers it

in 1951. Packed so tight, you swerve sideways
to your table. A full band on the stand.

The girl in front swaying with a chrome mic
bigger than your fist and telling you,

telling everyone, how much is lost
and what you have to do with and to each other

when you leave tonight, and soon.
No one knows yet how it will come out

and, just now, no one cares.
They care about the eyes that will not look away,

about the hand reaching across the table, about
the club, the song the club is soaked in—

the one they won't forget
when they cannot climb the stairs,

and the hand across the table is only a thought
while the daughter, who's made the soup

and holds the spoon and lifts it up,
pauses as those lips smile.

Coal Miner

—Bevier, Ky, 1931

for Joe Neal

If I am rich, I'm rich
in ways to die. There's lots
can kill you in a mine.
Gas, for a start—
Black Damp, Fire Damp,
Stink, and *White,* and *After Damp.*
Some smother, some explode
if a sledge and chisel
should conceive a spark.

The rock above your head
might elect at any moment
to shift a little closer
to the center of the planet.
The face of a wall or gallery
could scowl, take offense
at the blast and drill and chip
of emptiness worming through
and bulge, crumple,
slump.

A cousin died when
a mine mule kicked him
in the head. The cable
of the cage that hauls us
up and down could snap.
Or you can drown.
Drills punch through rock
find hidden rivers

thankful to be let loose.

And if you live to draw
that monthly check,
rock on the porch, ignore
the whistle, watch the boys
hustling to work,
what you did down there—
how you stooped to do it,
took a rock's clout or a broken beam's—
will twist your bones
like a bent-wood rocker.
You'll limp for mail
and to the company store
the way you did 400 feet
below the grass.

Water is merciful, quick
if you have to drown,
but not that dust
you breathe from your
first day, finer than
sand in an hourglass,
flakes of midnight
that sift into your lungs.

It could be ten or twenty years
until you grip the table
to get up from a chair
or two steps on the stairs,
stop to hunt your breath—
beat down, used up, worthless
as a clinker in a scuttle.

Eight months of the year.
Plain sunlight, simple breeze,

make a thin parenthesis,
a little slice on either side
of my dark day underground—
the morning and the evening walk
to and from the mine head
under the tipple's rattle.
Winter, I never see the light.
I rise and work and come
back home in dark.

Skinned like a rabbit
of my shirt and pants, I sit
cross-legged in a washtub
by the stove while my wife
pours water from the kettle
to wash away the murk.
From bed, I hear her drag
that soot-clogged, sloshing thing
out to the porch and dump it
in night's face. Mug's game,
but she persists.

I can hardly hum a tune,
so won't escape like some
I've known to stand on stages
in a dazzling suit behind
a guitar and a microphone.

I'll have no hole in the ground.
No stone, though relatives
be scattered close beside.
Nor be laid in a box
between two parlor chairs.
I've seen what I want
in a dream that comes back

like a friend to sit beside me
on the porch.

Carry me across that yellow
copperous-water creek, uphill,
through sassafras and sumac,
blackberry canes, to the clearing
sun hits first thing in the morning,
where you can watch it set.
A platform, locust, hickory,
higher than your head.

There I will lie, an offering
for buzzards. And it won't
be long before they funnel
down to dance and feast,
until my bones, picked clean
and polished by wind and sun
and rain, shine like the mantle
of a gas lamp pumped up tight.
And where they gleam
there won't be any dark.

Ravens

—Grandfather Mountain

The wind slams
against this spine
of rock the way long ago
hominins bashed one
chunk against another
hoping for a tool.

The mountain persists
from sheer contempt.
The ravens don't mind.
They like it up there
above the tree line
in the loud distance.

When the wind drops
you can hear their
corrugated grumbles
like boys dragging sticks
along a wooden fence

or the hocked-up
syllable or two they stole
from a work crew
on a ziggurat. They've
gathered on a slab
above the thrash of firs.

Hunchbacked. Shabby.
Coats the color of oil-
on-water. Of empty.
Of night in that story

you heard as a child.
They open their wings.
They lift from the rock
without a stroke.

My Civil War

1

Grant had a lot of buttons
on that coat—when he wore it.
Lee, as well. Blue. Gray. They
all did. Gold buttons. So many,
like gusts of sparks from a bonfire
up into a murderous, deluded
firmament. Still, they were men
you'd follow. Wanted to. Stiff hair.
Moustaches. Mutton chops.

Boys did—in flocks, in herds,
wagons, freight-cars full. Some
for honor. Some on principle.
Some for the uniform a girl
might fancy and lead them to
her bed. Some just to get away
from dirt-poor, hard scrabble to any
who-could-give-a-damn where.

The camps had speeches, songs,
cigars, baseball, decent coffee.
Store-bought and home-made
whiskey. Suttler's tents like
Ali Baba's cave on wagon wheels
when the sergeant counted out
your weekly pay. Girls who
smelled good and were easy as
your pockets when they were full.

Photographers—trunks packed
with knives long as your forearm,
pistols to brandish or poke into

your belt while you scowled half-
a-minute at the camera and mailed
the copy to the folks back home.
But what you didn't notice until
you saw the elephant, till formed
in a line, you walked into your first—

and shook and threw up
on the grass and kept on walking—
more afraid to stop, go back,
than to stumble on into that
whistling, dismembering air—

were the surgeons' tents ahowl
back of the line. The bloated, splayed
or peaceful as-if-sleeping dead, notes
in their pockets, pinned to jackets saying
where what's left should be sent.

And parts of bodies, heaps—
eskers and drumlins—the glacial
rubble as the battles moved away.
Undertakers—reeking chemicals,
carpenters hammering at coffins,
near the closest railhead.

And Gardener, his assistants posing
corpses before the grave details
had formed to dig. The darkroom
in his wagon developing the plates
he took and sent back to Brady's
DC studio to be hung so the public
might make some sense—might
take away a story from the wholesale
slaughter they'd lined up to see.

Three, four more years of this. Sun
down at Wilderness, the wounded
who couldn't crawl away died
screaming in brush fires that burned
all through the night. The hour, two,
at Antietam or Cold Harbor. Abattoirs
that left wreckage no pathologist,
no master butcher, could identify.

If not there, having the luck to miss
a bullet, you might die of gangrene,
typhoid, sepsis, cholera, dysentery
at Chimborazo or in Washington, before
a fever burned your mind away and
your heart or lungs surrendered or Walt
Whitman had the chance to write down
your last words and post them home.

2

I worked with a man whose
beard hung halfway down his chest—
a froth of muddy melting ice.
He dyed cloth with crushed walnut,
cut and sewed his uniform, made
his kit and drove hundreds of miles
on weekends to re-enact.

What is a country? Lines on a map—
across rivers, roads, fields?
Here? Not over there? Is it like
a family? Can anyone come in?

In that photograph—sepia (You've
seen it. You know the one I mean)—

along that town's muddy street,
the letters of the signs above the stores
are sharp. Tied at the rail, a horse
is rubbing his flank against a pole.
His tail is whisking flies. It's blurred.
The flag on the pole is blurred.

And I'm Not Making This Up

—with Marc Chagall

How did she escape the pages
of that Russian novel to confront me
in this Kroger parking lot?

Haystack frump, greatcoat, buttoned
to the kerchief knotted at her chin.
Kettle of grievance, rattling

from a long seethe of oppression.
She does not want directions
or a handout—just an ear.

But these Slavic gutturals rumbling
from some far storm and the pester
of consonants like fistfuls of gravel

raining on a door are lost on me.
Assaults like this can change a man.
As she fulminates, the pavement falls away

beneath my feet, becomes a lane and dirt.
Cars morph to wooden houses,
smoke from their chimneys squiggles

into the winter sky as I rise, afloat.
A goat smiles in my greening face.
The feather of a girl plays her violin.

The cow is milked. The man in the cloth cap
hurries home. From way up here I see
she takes a different road.

Her back, its beetle brown,
is bleached away in snow. Her scarf's
a wick, a flicking bit of red.

There are wolves in the drifts.
There are Cossacks in the shadows
of the pines. Their horses snort.

Snake Handling

When I was a boy
and came on one like a spool
of garden hose uncoiling,

I'd freeze—a fear-surge
of pennies on my tongue—the woods
gone white an instant till
that leaf-slither parting grass
rustled away.

A man I knew kept dozens
in the backyard minnow pool he'd drained.
I spent some summer afternoons
watching from its edge

that languid tangled bask
and carried off, deep into nights, things
gasping me awake.

It's years from there to here.
This room, built with sweat and cinder block,
by people I've known all my life—
here now on folding chairs because

they are afraid. Because they want
to hold the ones they've lost once more
and listen to the old words
they're too tired to read.

When it comes time, two men lug the box
Luther built from plywood scrap,
keeps in his shed out back and tends,
down the aisle and set it on the bench up front.

Someone reads. Someone prays.

At the nod, I rise and walk
in my clean, white shirt through hymns,
hand-clappings, wails, and heels
thumping floorboards

before I sink, elbows-deep, my arms
into that cool snarl—sluggish,
but wakening, twining
for the blood-throb's heat—

and lift above my head
the cursive writhing of the living word
I witness, but I cannot read.

Veteran's Day

—1954

They worked that day too,
a free catch-up, behind
the *CLOSED* sign on the door,
until the thump before the tune
from the high school band
shuffling up Main Street brought
them around from the garage,
out of the storeroom, from
behind the counter to stand
far back on the sidewalk
against the brick or glass
to watch above the heads
of children and their mothers
the colors pass, the scouts,
the girls waving from the back,
of the borrowed Chevrolet
convertible.
                    Unlike
the mayor and the judge and
the man who sells insurance—
still slim enough in his dress Blues
to fetch an admiral coffee—
they will not follow as that
small machine of noise turns
left at the courthouse, fades
downhill past the school
toward the edge of town.

They know that patch of stone
curbed grass, the dozen graves
away from family plots—not kin
by blood, but by the loss of it.

They know the vow when
cartridge weds the breech—
the consecrating bolt. They've
heard the volleys honor guards
aim at clouds.

The Long View

— for Preston and Shari

This morning we've passed
a patch of grass beside the creek
where his grandfather built and ran
a store, twisted a ways up a road,
parked, and found the weedy track,
choked with brush and deadfall,
to the burying ground—half
the size of a tennis court—hacked
vine and briar away until by noon,
we've found the stones. A dozen
and a half. Sagging, tipped, some
fallen, broken, the poorest crumbling
like stale loaves of bread. And
scattered in between, around, more
stoneless plots—dips, shallows
in the earth, like prints of thumbs
in dough, that catch the leaves.

He and his wife do this
a few times every year. Before
they leave this or that small place
he'll find the stone least legible,
weathered smooth as an old man's
memory, jot the name and date,
take it to the carver. And when
it's done, bring it back to set up
where the old one was.

He doesn't farm much anymore,
puts in a garden every spring,
mows the field along the road
when it seems to need it. Trees

have his attention now. He'll cut
one now and then, sell the board
or make a table or a cabinet
in his shop.

This afternoon—
around the hill, across the field,
beyond the barn—we walk his back
woodlot. Kicking through the leaves,
we don't say much. We've known
each other close to sixty years. We've
said most of what we have to say.
For him, these woods are like a
family. He knows these trees like
cousins. He stops in front of one—
a walnut, thicker than a phone pole
and my waist.

In fifty years, he says,
there'll be some good wood there.

II

Indian Summer

Somewhere up in the oak
the party's over.

A rubble of acorns
popping underfoot like
tired balloons.

The air so still.

Hardly a wrinkle on the pond.
The late light falling.

No. Floating through the trees.
Yellow. Gold.

Offering the leaves another choice
besides this worn-out green

and a way to tumble
when they can't hold on.

First frost? A week or two
until it tries a gloss, a little silver,
for an hour on the grass.

And tries again next day
until it gets it right.

October

High in the pines wind,
practicing for winter,
bellows a wake-up call

over the neighborhood
before it dives into backyards
mugging hydrangeas,

pummeling asters. Red
and yellow maples make
a glowing tunnel of the street.

Bright leaves scuttle
gutter to gutter, huddle
against the curb.

Like soldiers in the trenches,
they know no one
gets out of this alive.

Snowfall All Night

—New Mexico

You hear it the way the Inuit hear
high shimmering draperies crinkling
the dark, the way stars whisper

to the San like coals mumbling
on a hearth. A month ago, aspen
quivered, rattled like a dancer's gourd.

Now this handiwork's progressing
north before dawn, high and away—
Wyoming... Saskatchewan.

Stand beyond the fan of light
from the kitchen door, farther than
a checkbook, next month's rent,

until the house means nothing
and you're somewhere harsher, wider,
wilder, following food by track and scat.

Where anything means more
than everything behind. Where hunger
sets a table finer than any feast.

Snow

Out of this fierce world
with its indifferent sky,
how with such delicacy
can such mildness come?

And you in the center
of this whisper—out late
to greet it with your breath
one white word at a time.

A temporary treaty between
contending summer greens—
bushes you've clipped, grass
you've mown most of a year.

The shed, the fence, a stump.
The whole of it smoothed to
pure curves by this incremental
blanketing of everything.

Less than a purr, stroking
it quiet, calming whatever
cries out from its dream,
turning it back to sleep.

No script.
No lines in the playbook
you can speak. Your part in this
is standing there.

January from a Window at Sunset

The flush of leaving's
what we notice most—
thus, the white glint
of a steeple on the ridge
across the river under
a sky preparing for stars,
wisps of cloud alchemizing
pink to orange. All miracle,
not least for not involving
us, who under this, in this,
take it for granted, else
meet madness or find God.
We have a lot to lose
and we will some season.
Meantime these bare trees
to which the birds come
back—filling the branches
the way from dreams
from sleep each morning
we come back to ourselves.

Spring

Before it's
anywhere it's
in the air

for your nose to assess
like a buyer

strokes cloth
between a thumb
and finger. And

you want more:
bolts, warehouses, ships'
holds of it,

freighters full.
Down by the creek
a bird.

(It's always a bird
and curious.)

Even if you knew
as much as he does
the stream would

still shush, is shushing
steadily. Ripples

like lost scarves
crumpling sunlight. The
rocks underneath

happy to gleam as
stones in a ring.

Alders and winged
elms. Buds tipping
every twig.

The tiniest green of
not-yet leaves

the shape of candle
flames

in a quiet room.
Light coming earlier.
Staying later.

Dark shrinking
like a sweater
in a dryer.

And the leaves.
Not yet lit. But
almost.

March

Any other month,
you'd

call the cops,
report

this noise from
that backyard

party way out of
hand.

The buck and toss
of everything.

Upthrusting
gusts. Shrubs

shaking like
soaked dogs.

Half-leaved
trees, fringingly

green. Knouts
flailing—nothing

to lash.
Boisterous assaults

of roil
sinking in a second

to a whisper.
All this

out on new grass
under

a dome of cloud
and blue.

Galliards of
wind and tree,

of air and
green. The engine

of the hugest
machine—

up on blocks and
idle for a while

is cranking,
turning over.

Feel the thrum,
the throb?

It's pulling
away from the curb,

taking you as
far as summer,

as far as
fall.

Sometimes a Day Gets Lost

wanders away from April maybe
or late September. It arrives
without papers, itself its own
passport. In the gutters,
leaves are confused. What
was escape is play. It is enough
to make trees dream, erupting
green. Out of the blue, light
falls through crystal, soft,
breeze nuzzling everything.

An equal opportunity miracle
like some ripe galleon blown
off course, split open on a reef,
scatters glittering tonnage
over the sand or the way you
wandered along that street one
afternoon into the little shop,
chock-a-block with nothing
you'd ever want, lifted something
from a shelf and looked at me.

Lot's Wife

Messengers of God, the two strode
like torches into the hills. The town was tinder,
a fuse they'd lit. Dust, small stones, their steps
in the scorched grass asked too much of her.
She winced at the flames that were their wings.

The narrator has pace to consider
and the fate of the chosen. In a single line,
he turns, as she turned away,
leaving her on the brow of the hill
squinting to read the few words of the verse
her doorposts added to the great black scroll
unrolling above the plain, and wept herself
empty. The hot wind sweeping past
fixed her in the crust of her own salt.

Through Zoar and beyond, evening, as it had to,
sifted down. Scrawny mountain cattle came.
With many soft carvings their tongues took what was left.
They do not forget. Each night they come home,
Their delicate mouths bearing her grief.

The Cunning to Get Near Enough

Curve of road, shape of hill,
easy things that come when my eyes call.

A stick at a time I've fed small miracles,
frightening the loud night,

as the fog lifts in a clearing gone to blackberry,
given my last breath, least movement,

for the moment when what crops the wet grass
fades over the creek into the hemlocks.

But this woman, humming
as in a kitchen where everything's used

and has its place, opens again and again
the heart to see how it is rising.

Fingers

In touch with doorknobs, gearshifts, buttons, brushes, forks,
high-handed, almost, for them, things are a snap—and yet

they burrow in my pockets examining both sides of coins,
find no key, run through my hair, come back empty-handed.

I give them pages to turn, shirts to fold, plates to scrape.
We go for a walk. Cupped around nothing, they forget,

swing for a while at my sides like kids at the playground,
then clench and trace the worn maps of my palms.

Good at counting, they count, eliminate—sure it'll turn up
among scissors, paperweights, rubber bands, corkscrews,
broomsticks.

They plunge into the dishwasher, lose themselves in laces,
latches, handles, zippers, buckles, gloves, pliers.

It's late. They strike matches, the laptop's keys,
fret and pick at guitar strings. Clearly, things aren't adding up.

They fidget on the desk like a nervous chorus line,
dither with a pencil. Nothing left to tally, they quit.

Toothpaste capped, the light flicked off,
they trail at length over a countryside of sheets.

What good to say be patient, she'll be back,
airy shapes for the dark, nothing they can grasp.

Curling, bewildered, they churn like damned rivers
at the ends of my arms reaching for you, the sea.

Hamada's Bowl

About the size of
the same color as cupped
hands lifting water
from a stream.

I've seen it speak
just enough rice
cloud-white and steaming.
Soup. Wine. Five cool plums
ripening.

Hamada made it.
Soft clay. Slow wheel.
Lifting from a lump
this gesture fire fixed.
Glazed as if left out
in the rain.

When I kiss you,
this is the way I want
to hold your face.

This bowl's the face
I'd like to see each morning
in my mirror.

When nothing fills me
or too much, I'd
like to hold it.
I'd like to offer it
like this.

Sumerian

She
spoke
a dialect of
Sumerian all
gutturals and
honey

Her
headdress
full of birds and
lightning

How
she moved
around that room
the way her gown
swept
everything
was

more than
any dream could
hold

Broke like an
egg

Slimed the dawn

Nowhere
I walked that day

that did not
gleam
that was not
sheathed

with that bright
slick.

Muse

—for Euterpe

Once
there were
long, acrobatic
nights
that left me
short of breath
on sweat-wet
sheets.

My Sweet
and *follow me*—
no bathrobes,
slippers—
to the shower,
back to bed.

Years now
postcards come,
licentious scrawls,
illegible
almost.

Something
I said?
Commutes
from Helicon
too long?

I'd trade any
late-night
dream

for her tongue's
wake-up call
tracing my ear.

No questions,
bathrobes,
slippers,
just that whisper:
Follow me.

III

Redwoods Up the North Coast

—for Lucas

The farther north we drove, the fewer
the fields, the fences tumbled, gapped,
the trees taller, crowding down from the
coast range, the lower the sky and grayer,
the broader the Pacific, the horizon
farther, until the light, absent-minded
all afternoon, finally forgot before
Lucas found the dirt track and turned
from the immensely mumbling ocean
following the headlights up the gulch
into the grove. Parked when the road
quit. Went by flashlight along the creek
through bracken and undergrowth.
Moving from room to greater rooms
whose walls were mist and ceilings fog.
And came among those trees—each an
epoch with its origin and history, rising
into night. Were admitted without papers,
into that chastening quiet suggesting
we put aside small noises we might make
in favor of the ancient grammar
of that silence.

So, slept like mayflies—cocooned
in down and nylon—and dreamt away
quick time for another measured out
in single droplets seeded from thick air,
swelling pearl-slow on rhododendron leaves
until inching to the edge and falling,
they tapped the leaf below. And the tinge
of that other pace lingered like woodsmoke

in a sweater when we woke, packed, and
hiked out speechless. On up the road,
the silent woman at the store behind
the single pump must have felt it too when
she made change. And it was farther still
before one of us, sipping from a steaming
paper cup remembered the word for *coffee*
and the word for good.

How the Second Violin Played

four days
out from Southampton
decorating air for first class
diners and the loungers
outside the café at the foot
of the Grand Stair.

A quartet and a trio
hardly more than boys, but
seasoned from recitals, music halls,
orchestra pits.

The White Star gig's a plum
for him. New tux, folding money,
the cabin finer than his room
back in Dundee.

After a cheroot, the sherry
in the lounge, he's in his berth.

Asleep.

Three decks above,
for the lookout in the crow's nest
near the bow, the sea's
obsidian. Calm, utterly. Sky onyx,
light years deep.

Stars

as if the Bursar's safe
has been cracked and rifled.
Diadems, tiaras, bracelets, chokers,

necklaces broken apart, stones
scattered, strewn wholesale
across the dome above.

The sea below—its twin
reflected—makes a globe in which
and always at the center of
the ship steams. And at the seam
where the half-spheres meet,

a speck

vagrant, tiny, white—mild
in the distance, with space
and calm and time
enough to grow—

grows as it nears,
slowly becomes, from arctic cold
and water heaped,

a mountain

until below the waterline
it strokes the starboard flank
and slits the hull, compartment
by compartment, plate
by plate.

That shiver doesn't wake him,
hardly rocks the bunk.
It's the steward's knuckles
rapping the door
with captain's orders to report.

He does.

And in that simmer of confusion
the quartet and the trio
meld. Began to play
as Rostron, Captain of Carpathia
(steaming for them, hours late)
would say

it is the duty "... of the Ship's
band, in an emergency, to play
to calm the passengers."

Lively tunes. (No one
recalls *Nearer My God to Thee.*
Some remember *Alexander's*
Ragtime Band.)

They play an hour
and half an hour more until the bow,
welcoming water like a doorman bribed,
cants, lifting the fantail—
a promontory with the best of views

for the strew of white boats
standing off, moving away,
like peaked napery abandoning
the dining rooms.

And from the boats,
the ship itself—the rising,
tipping of it, deck lights, portholes
blazing against the hull's black—
is a constellation dismissed
from the sky, slipping star
by star away.

They keep the tempo
while the deck forgets ideas
of level, stand as panicked chairs
desert, skidding away
down polished teak.

They play until
there is no standing.
No *da capo.* Until wood
underfoot is water.

Until the violin unmoored
from the harbor of his hands
sets out with the cargo
of its songs.

Money Well Spent

—Bach at St. Thomas

After the court
at Danzig turned him
down, he never tried again,
settled in, turned to
what he could do best—
music and children.

Leipzig
had no prince, no bishop,
no opera house. Still
it was respectable—
a position and a church.
He wheedled and cajoled,
cobbled together choirs on
what the Elders parted with.

In good dark cloth,
burghers filled the pews—
hard men beneath those
bellies, keeping sharp eyes
on their tithes.

God had been good to them.

Pious and proud,
honor-bound to fill the
contract's terms, they sit
in what their labor's
wrought while the master
at the console spins new
heavens from the stunned,

enchanted air above heads
reckoning the price of swine
and corn, the cost to plug
the transept's leak.

Truly, I tell you,
they have their reward.

A Photograph of Mandelstam at Thirty-One

Somewhere in that room steam
begins to puff like breath from the spout
of the kettle on the hissing primus.
Soon a friend will offer you a biscuit and hot tea.

But first the shutter of the camera in his hand
must slam shut like a cell door
so we can see how, already, your captive face
is turning away, how shadow dusts your forehead,
how well your eye has mastered the exile's stare.

Here no one believes he can say anything
dangerous enough to be locked up for.
Our stomachs are full. Snow does not
lean on our houses. Even so,
we have tracked you word by word a little way
across the steppes

and sit now, tonight, remembering how you say *bread,*
a loaf you've earned.
Say *stove.* We will huddle around.
Hand us the word *glass*
trembling as if it would spill out of itself.

The Living Corpse

Tallahassee (AP) With a rock band blaring in the background and a crowd of 100 at graveside, Bill White was buried six feet under Saturday—for the forty-ninth time. White is trying to resume his trade as a living corpse. . . .

Forty-nine times I've done this—enough to lie
down under strings of lights and plastic
streamers, ignoring my eulogy, to be
nailed in and lowered while bystanders
applaud the hole the management provides
for its attraction, me, hoping to sell
a few more cheeseburgers or cars. The first dirt
strikes the lid like buckshot on a tin roof,
but soon it's covered, and the sound recedes—
a woman with a broom, sweeping her way
to the far end of the hall—and the dim
drumming of the crowd's feet wanders away.

I have a light, a radio, a phone
for company. For a week, disc-jockeys
call. *Brothers and sisters,* they say, *tonight*
Rick's rappin' with a stiff. Can you dig it?
This peters out. A governor called once
to wish me luck, and a heavy breather.
Next, it's the drunks, slurring their messages
to the grave. And last come the abandoned,
the lonely—women with husbands gone all night.

Their shy voices hope for answers. *What's it like?*
they ask.
        Dark, I say, *and cramped.*

Why
do you do it?
It's a living, I say. Or, *For*
practice.
They laugh at this, and I can hear
a room with too much empty space echo
that laugh. And I can see them in terry-
cloth robes worn thin, hair wound in rollers,
perched on the edge of too much bed.

I thank them and hang up and do not say
how many rooms I've paced to find out what
I need or how my own lost tunnel through
the dark to scrabble at the plywood boards
and whisper to me with the same old voice—
my own. But you can't stay dead for long.

Comes a day I leave it all down there
with roots and grubs and fat, slack worms.
There is a resurrection and a band.
The MC on the platform claps my shoulder,
proclaims a record, and hands me the check
while I shift on legs forgotten so long
they're new, and the curious faithful applaud
my face as it sways in the dazzling light.

Some Angels

I think of them as muscle.

At somebody's cousin's restaurant.
The south side. Cicero.

A nice place
where they never pay.

Waiters, tense against the wall
alert for a nod, a glance.

Something *Bolognese*
with the proprietor's best red.

Those suits, shiny as celestial armor
in storage temporarily,

capacious, loose, accommodating
bellies, chests, wings.

When they finish the cannoli,
it's time to go.

If, by accident, design,
they find you,

the third-floor walk-up,
at a hotplate stirring soup—

nudged by a holy shoulder,
forgetting locks and hinges,

the door will lie down flat in adoration.
Cracking knuckles, they'll commence.

And that sad room will ring as if
it were a bell, your skull the clapper,

till it explodes with color, shaming
any patriotic detonations in a velvet sky

above the harbor on a holiday. If
you wake up, you'll have a tale to tell

that will make strangers
on park benches slide away

leaving you to feed the pigeons
by yourself. If it were me

I'd keep my big mouth shut (with its
split lip, broken tooth, that penny-tang—

blood on the tongue). We know
what happens to a snitch. Who'd guess

what the Big Guy has in mind?

Day Day

—for David Morris

His name was David
but that was one too many syllables
for him to say. He'd try.
Tried hard—the way you'd coax
an engine on a winter morning,
the way the needle on an LP,
knocked back by a scratch,
tries again.

We took him at his word
those days we clotted along College Street
and walked to school.

Day-Day it was. No malice,
only the way you'd call a redhead
Rusty or *Carrot-top.* And he laughed
the way we did.

But mostly he was quiet, smiling
at how the words streamed water-smooth
spilling from us on the playground
or trickled from the back of class.

Miss Wells gave him a break,
but when she'd nod and call,
he'd stand a long time by his desk
mulling the answer while we'd wait.

He was good at dodgeball,
kick the can. Better, later, at baseball,
basketball. And better still at sawing,

planing, sanding, painting,
in Mr. Hughes' shop.

No problem with his brain.
He saw clearly what he had to say—
that landscape, rolling down
toward a river, up again, the meadows,
trees, the hills, rising beyond.

But the path across those fields
was potholed, full of faulters, trips, and stumbles,
choked with rubble ... stones. ...

I can't say how long it took, how much
clambering, how many stops and starts,
but he got where he meant to go.

Last time I saw him
I was teaching for the state.
He was driving trucks out at the mines.
We talked and drank our beer.

After an Old Chinese Poet

The Ministry still runs.
Those boys, preening
new beards, will learn
their trade or not
and, like so many old
friends, spend careers
in the dusty West
dodging Tartars' arrows
or far South where thieves
and tigers tax the province
and snooze in the jungle's
tangled green.

The Sons of Heaven
follow one another
into the tomb like
ducks to the pond.
The business here is
crops, weather, children,
and children's children
on holidays.

Who could want more
than a little pension,
a ratty gown, and one hundred
codgers like yourself?
A few close at hand
on the verandah, the rest
asleep in scrolls,
their songs less now
than the moon's light
as it begins its climb.

Somebody plays the lute.
Somebody sings. You
drag your sleeve
in the bowl of wine
following the moon
where it always goes.

To the Dogs

—for Craig Stangohr

You get old, you get soft
from the inside out,
like a peach in a dish on the table
before the bruises show.

I'm binge-watching YouTube videos—
the ones the rescue shelters post
hoping for donations.

Dogs. Mostly.
Those wolf-clever creatures
who, way back when, took a chance
and cast their lot with us.

The plots are simple as an apple,
as the fat crayons and gray paper
Mrs. Bryant handed out
when it was coloring time.

Abandoned, beaten, starved,
mutilated randomly, these cowerings are lifted
out of ditches, heaps of trash, or coaxed
from brambles, alleys, from under cars
or houses, finally, with bits of kibble
to the leash and cage.

Ride to the vet's, the gentle prods—
a bath, bowl of fresh water, decent food,
a clean, new bed.

And in a month (the denouement)

the curled-between-the-back-legs tail
is full of wags.

It's working.

I'm channeling the heart
of some actress, ancient and forgotten
decades up the coast,
down the dirt road, beyond the gate,
to her rescued menagerie—feathered, furred,
great, and small. The peaceabl-est kingdom
where the healed and healing are redeemed.

When I share over a drink—
mention this—she laughs and says,

Oh, the Humanity!

You always were a traitor
to your kind.

And she may be right
of me, of us, on two legs fewer
and a good bit farther from the ground...
teetering, snout-first, into miracle,
exhaling good and ill like CO2
with every step.

My Rolodex long gone.
The contacts on my phone—
addresses, numbers—everything wiped clean.
Only the list of names.

Where is my scattered pack
no howl can reach?

Dream Dreams

your young men shall see visions and
your old men shall dream dreams
—Acts 2:17

Passed him early, at the railing
in the middle of the old bridge downtown.
Sky clear as water in a bedside glass.
The last fat stars. Downriver, east still dark.

No jumper (from the parka and binoculars
around his neck) and likely, no Tom
out peeping at the few lit windows of the high-
rise where I'd guess he lives. Most likely
only a fitful sleeper like myself, up early,
shedding the lint of dreams.

He's facing upstream, pondering,
maybe, the river's etiology, how it unbraids,
frays back toward one hundred streams and springs.

A younger man might face the other way,
lean at the opposite rail, watch downriver
where, when the seam along the east ignites,
new visions will compose themselves.
But he stays put, although binoculars
can't be much use just now.

Maybe he's waiting for a few more
jots and tittles of the coming light, enough
to glimpse the water's cursive whispers
flowing below. Enough finally to make out
birds roosting on the branches, in the sedge
along the bank. To watch them
waking to their only day.

Wishbone

Pulley bone we called it.
You won't find it
in the bucket or the box
from a fast-food place.

It comes trilling from a cast-
iron-skillet-Crisco-seethe
to drizzle glisten on a paper towel
before it finds the plate
of the oldest or the youngest
in that room.

And if that little slingshot—
crisp and gold—came to you
and you gnawed it smooth,
you'd hold it out,
offering a tine to someone
for you both to bend
until it snapped.

I don't recall if the one
who held the shortest or the longest
splinter got the wish.
There was a way to cheat,
but I've forgot that too.

I have one now, between
my slick forefinger and my thumb.
Around this table they're all here
disguised as air. I hold it up.

And if I break it,
will I half-win? Will it mean
that I'll get half a wish

or that that wish will come
half-true?

Still, I bend it till it snaps.
I know who they are.
They know what I wish.